treasuring
everyday
joy™

with
Johnson's®

photography by
michael franzini

make a promise...

The JOHNSON'S® Team knows that the demands of day-to-day life can consume all your thoughts and attention, especially since parents today are busier than ever. That's why we set out on a mission to connect with families across the country to find out: How does America find joy in the everyday?

We traveled from coast-to-coast, spending time with one family in each state to get an inside glimpse at what parenthood is really like across America. We discovered a common theme in every home: raising a child is about more than just the "firsts," it's about a collection of special moments that fill each and every day. If you pause and reflect, you'll recognize the simple joys that already exist in your everyday life— the gleeful grin from your baby in the bathtub, the feeling of those sticky fingers reaching out for your hand. Join us in treasuring these simple pleasures by celebrating the everyday joy around you.

Make a promise to step back, be present, and discover the joy in each and every day.

Good Morning, Sunshine

We might soak our baby up a bit more than most. My husband Shelton and I had a six-year fight with infertility, which we chronicled on our in vitro fertilization (IVF) fundraiser blog. With help from generous people who read our blog, we successfully completed IVF in 2009 and Paisley was born in April 2010! The best five minutes of our entire day are in the morning. We wake up to Paisley chattering to herself on the baby monitor, then we bring her back to our bed and cuddle up together while we give her the bottle. It's a really great moment that exists in this little "pod" in our room.

Those few minutes in the morning, when it's just the three of us, that is when we know the in vitro shots and the tears and the money and the waiting were all worth it. I don't think, even on the days that we longed for her the most desperately, that we thought it would be quite this good. This is what we waited for all those years.
—Brandi Koskie, Paisley's Mom

Nathan, 2 years
The Buckley Family
Nevada

Mixing with Mom

In the morning, most of the life in our house is in the kitchen where Nathan and I are making breakfast. It's our favorite time of the day, because it's the one time we're always together as a family. Blueberry pancakes are a family favorite and Nathan loves being the mixer. The batter ends up all over his hands, face and sometimes the floor. Nathan is always beaming when we sit down for breakfast. My husband Sterling and Nathan's brother and sister tell him how delicious the meal is and he is so proud to have helped. The lost batter and clean up are well worth the smiles and laughs the two of us share.
—Sara Buckley, Noah, Madeline, and Nathan's Mom

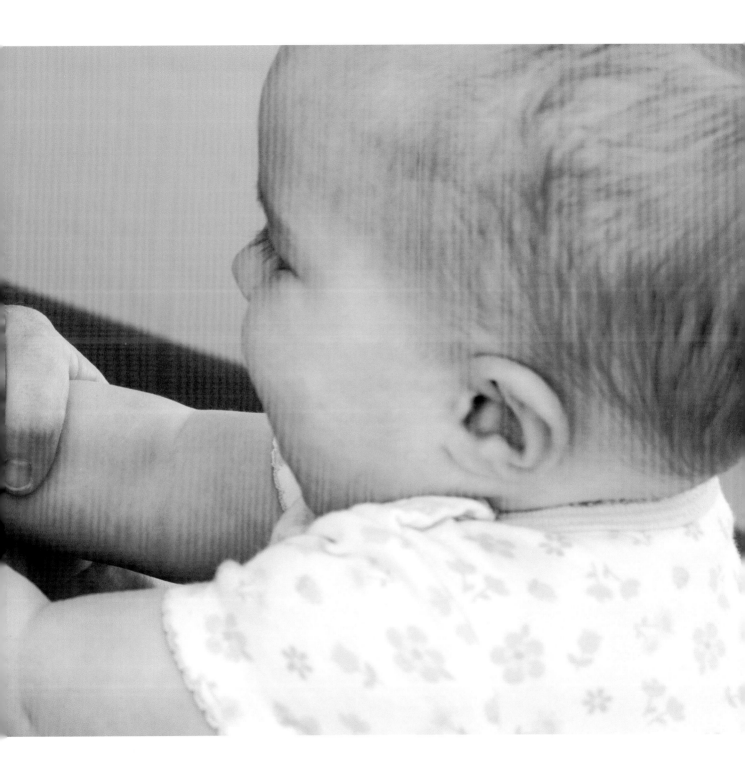

Lucy, 9 months
The Rapp Family
Arizona

Wake-up Call

I work nights in the police force and don't get home until late. In the morning, my wife Julie plops our daughter Lucy on my chest to wake me up. Even if I've had a rough shift, I can't be grumpy with this little ball of joy on my chest. Lucy is the first thing I see in the morning, which makes me wake up with a smile. My life is a whole lot sunnier with her in it. My job is very dangerous so I make sure to hug and kiss my family everyday before I go to work. These sweet moments with my kids, Cruz, Luke, and Lucy, remind me of the simple pleasures of life. I leave for work all filled up with positive energy.

—Andy Rapp; Cruz, Luke, and Lucy's Dad

Reese, 6 months
The von Storch Family
Arkansas

Baby in the Mirror

The blessing of our sweet baby girl is one of the most amazing gifts my husband Andy and I have ever received. Every day is a new adventure—we explore new sights and sounds together with her. We love to watch the wonder in her eyes and the joy that comes when she learns something new.

I love to hold Reese up to the mirror because she doesn't recognize that it is her own reflection yet. That little girl in the mirror is Reese's best friend and her face lights up every time she sees her. She'll lean closer and closer to catch a glimpse of the baby on the other side of the glass. Then she'll break out into a huge grin when she finally sees her. Reese is just wonderful. My husband and I had always wanted children and a family, but because we didn't meet until later in life, we weren't sure if it would happen for us. We are just so thrilled that we were able to have the family we wanted after all.

—Janelle von Storch, Reese's Mom

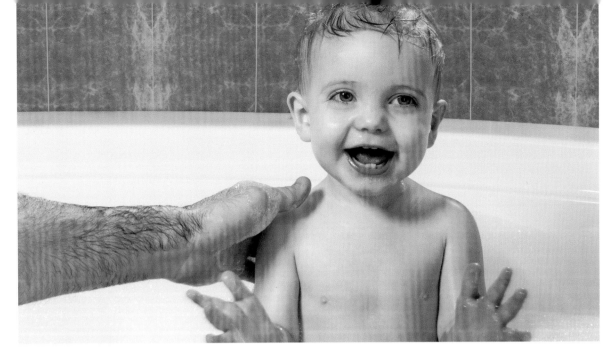

Taylor, 1 year
The Hill Family
Utah

Bubble Beard

As a busy dad, I try to find time to spend with each of my kids one-on-one. Bath time is the perfect way for me to bond with my son Taylor. He loves playing with the bubbles, so I try to make as many as possible. Taylor likes to make car sounds and drive his rubber ducky through the mounds of bubbles. Lately, Taylor has been taking the suds from the bath and making himself a sudsy white beard. When he is finished piling them on, he looks up and points at my chin. When I feel my face and act surprised that my goatee is there, he erupts in hysterical laughter. Laughing with my son is the perfect way to end the day.
—Tracy Hill; Kennadi, McKinlee, and Taylor's Dad

Kinsley, 1 year
The Ramey Family
Kentucky

Taekwondo Kid

My fiancé Sean grew up learning Taekwondo; now he is the master at his school and is able to pass on his knowledge to the local kids. Now that Kinsley is in our lives, Sean loves to have her involved in the school and can't wait to teach her Taekwondo one day too! We love watching Kinsley's excitement watching the students kick and Ki-Hup. Sean and I enjoy the thought of one day passing on the tradition of Taekwondo to our baby girl. For now, seeing her all dressed up in her mini Taekwondo outfit, grinning from ear to ear and playing on the mats, is all we need!

—Christy Satterley, Kinsley's Mom

Jace, 1 ½ years
The Batiste Family
Louisiana

Squirms, Wiggles, and Giggles

Jace loves lotion time so much. After his bath, he will go get his own special blue blanket and bring it to me so that I can put lotion on him. I'll lay him down on his blanket on the living room floor and start by rubbing his belly. He is very ticklish. As soon as I start touching his ribs, he just starts to laugh. Then I move on to his arms and legs. Jace loves it as he squirms, wiggles, and giggles. When I first told my grandma what I was doing with Jace, she told me she used to do the same thing with me when I was little. That just makes our lotion time even more special.
—Ontranekia Nixon, Jace's Mom

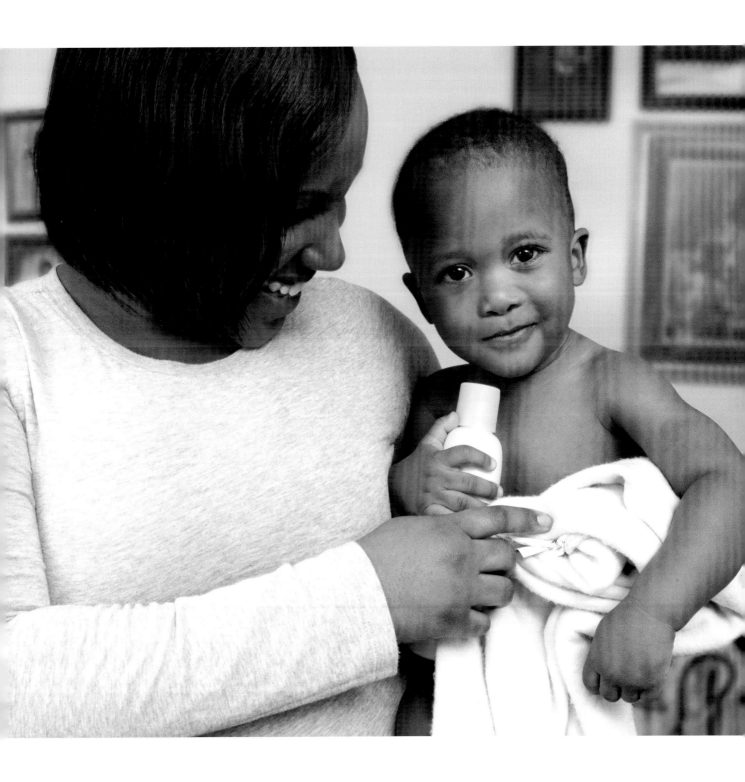

 Elijah, 9 months
The Turner Family
California

Disappearing Toes

Elijah loves the beach! He is particularly fascinated by the sand. My husband Daniel and I love to help him bury his toes in it. He loves the feeling of the warm sand on his feet, although after a little while he'll start to look troubled that his toes have disappeared. That's when I'll pull him up a little and say "Peek-a-boo!" as they reappear. He'll giggle wildly and then hide his toes again for another round.

—Jessica Turner, Elijah's Mom

Puppy Love

Addison loves Miley, our family dog, and has taken it upon herself to care for her. Every morning, Addison races into the kitchen and grabs Miley's bowl and food. She pours the food, but most of it misses the bowl, and it ends up on the floor. Then she stands by Miley's side, joyfully watching her puppy gobble up breakfast. The first few times Addison fed her, I was worried about her dropping the food everywhere, but I relaxed when I saw how proud Addison was of her new responsibility.

My husband Greg and I got Miley for Addison on her second birthday, and they have been best friends ever since. Addison loves to hold her—she'll put the dog in her lap and they'll sit there for hours. It's wonderful to see my daughter shower our puppy with so much love.
　　　　　　　　—Natalie Parsons, Addison's Mom

Kito, 11 months
The Turner Family
Oklahoma

Drummer Boy

When I was pregnant with my son Kito, he used to kick and kick and kick, so I would joke, "He's going to come out playing the drums!" Sure enough, Kito is my little drummer boy. He likes to crawl up to a chair with a comb or a brush and beat on the seat like it's a drum set. My mom and I sing to him, and Kito drums along. My little drummer boy lights up my life.
—Keenya Turner, Kito's Mom

Reina, 2 ½ years
The Sexton Family
Rhode Island

Fairy Princess

Reina is a girly girl who loves to play dress up. She has a couple of little princess dresses and a tutu skirt with wings. What Reina wears depends on her mood. She has a little vanity set and she goes the whole nine yards. We play together and she dresses me up as well. I'll say "Reina, I want to wear the dress!" and she'll say, "Oh mommy, you don't fit in the dress." So, she'll put jewelry on me instead. I think we have such a strong bond since I am a single mom and we're always together. She's like my little partner in crime. She's my little fashionista who's always by my side.

—Lynn Sexton, Reina's Mom

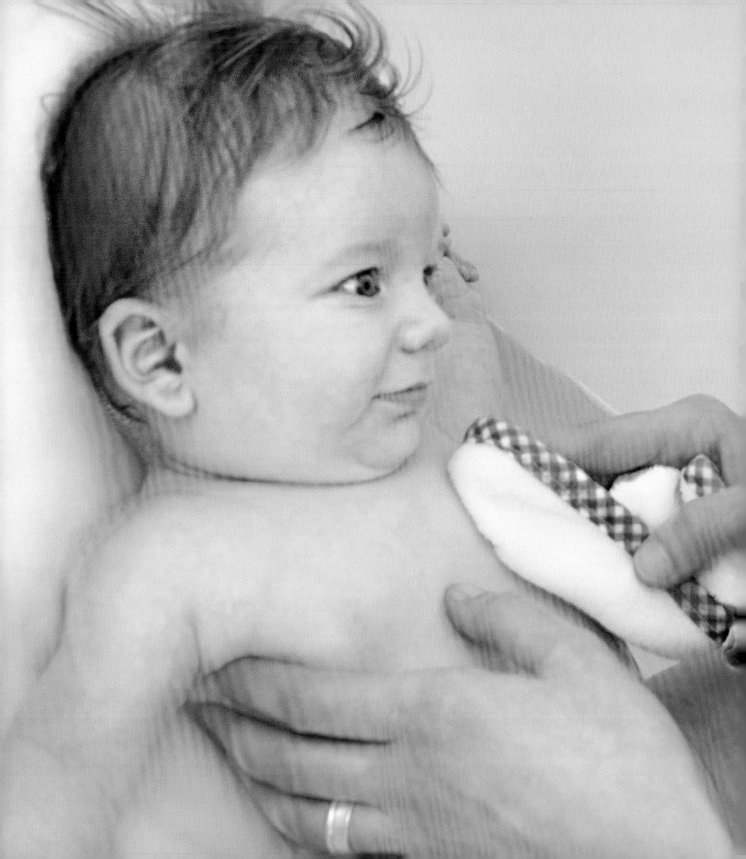

Ezra, 9 weeks
The Satz Family
Vermont

Homegrown

My husband Jon and I live on a farm not far from where I was raised. Coming back to Vermont to raise my own family made me appreciate how great it was growing up here; I know our son Ezra will love it just as much. While giving Ezra baths in our kitchen sink, I look out the window and imagine where he will play and what his favorite places will be. It's the perfect setting to enjoy seeing Ezra so happy in the water, learning to kick and splash. I couldn't imagine a better place to raise our son. The farm has so much more life in it now that Ezra is around!
—Courtney Satz, Ezra's Mom

Maryn, 2 years
The Yunker Family
Minnesota

Tiny Dancer

Maryn loves her tutus—and has a ton of them. She wears a tutu in the house, on errands around town, and sometimes she even asks to sleep in them. She would wear them all the time if she could! Maryn loves to dance, but I don't know where she gets her material from. She twirls in circles, putting her arms out like a ballerina. When my husband James and I take Maryn to our health club, she dances to the music they play in the hallways. As she jumps around and twists in circles, other members can't help but laugh and smile. She's such a character. I love to see her dancing around all over the place!
—Ann Marie Yunker, Maryn's Mom

Braden, 1 ½ years
The Zuker Family
Tennessee

Mommy's Helper

When it comes to cleaning, Braden is my little helper. I am not allowed to vacuum without him. He likes me to push it toward him and runs away laughing. I swear he drops things on purpose, like cereal, just because he knows we will get the vacuum. Then he'll go "Uh-oh!" and show you where the vacuum is. When I bring it out, he always offers to help. I'm not sure how much he actually does, but he sure loves to try!

Braden literally adores anything cleaning-related. He loves the feather duster and will go around dusting things with it. At restaurants, he will take a napkin and start wiping his chair off, whether there's anything there or not. He is obsessed with cleaning. The vacuum is his favorite cleaning aid though. Once he sees it, that's it, he just wants to vacuum. I'm sure he'll grow out of it when he's older and my husband David and I want him to clean, but for right now he has a blast. Even if it takes more time to let him "help" me, I don't mind. I'd vacuum for days if it meant making my son happy.

—Shannon Reagan, Braden's Mom

Avri, 2 years
The Ludwig Family
Alaska

Family Fort

Avri loves building forts with my husband Chet and me. We hang blankets over the couch and toy box. He likes to hide in the forts like it's his very own little getaway. We give him time alone to explore and use his imagination, but sometimes we can't help but crawl in there and play with him! We play hide-and-seek behind the toy box, I peek my head around it and Avri laughs every time. It might not be hard to do, but making our little guy laugh is my favorite thing in the world. Spending time in the forts gives us a chance to escape from the everyday and just be a happy, laughing family. I love every minute of it.

—Sara Ludwig, Avri's Mom

Shotta, 2 years
The Tyson Family
Connecticut

Hoops

My brother Shotta loves to play with his mini basketball hoop inside the house. He plays every time he sees a ball—and thinks everything is a ball. He will even pick up grapefruits and throw them around. There are a lot of us in the house and we all play with him; he shoots ball the entire day. We all like to cheer him on and he loves that! He gets so excited when he makes it in, he does a little victory dance. Actually he gets excited even when he doesn't make it in! He makes everybody laugh with his little dances. He's always smiling and there's nothing like his smile to warm our hearts.

—Azria Rountree, Shotta's Sister

Three Little Miracles

When Ray and I heard we were having triplets, I just about fell off the ultrasound table. At first I thought, "There's no way we can handle three babies." My second thought was, "I just hope they're all healthy." We soon found out there were some serious complications with my pregnancy. The triplets were born 13 weeks premature. Caleb came first at 2.4 pounds, Andrew was 1.9 pounds, and finally James at 2.8 pounds. Each baby was given less than a 50 percent chance for survival. The boys fought for every breath in the NICU, but eventually we brought them all home!

We came up with a way to help our friends and family tell the boys apart—we color coded them. Caleb was blue, Andrew was red, and James was green. Color coding is now a part of everything we do, from decorating their bedrooms to getting them dressed. All three boys are improving every day. In order to help families avoid premature birth and time in the NICU, we signed up to be the ambassador family for the MARCH OF DIMES® in South Carolina. It means the world to us to be able to give other families hope through sharing our story. I'm so thankful for my three boys. Knowing that they weren't even supposed to make it out of the hospital makes every moment of every day with our boys that much more precious.
    —Tori Billings; Caleb, Andrew, and James' Mom

Great Outdoors

Our house has a huge back deck, and it's our favorite place to spend time as a family. We have a perfect view of the Boise skyline and love to watch the sunset from the deck together. My husband Michael and I enjoy the quality time we get to spend with our girls, Isabella and Chloe, outdoors.

Chloe, our youngest, really lights up when we're on the deck. I love seeing her look around with her eyes open wide, checking everything out. She is particularly fascinated by the leaves blowing in the wind. When we're outside and Chloe feels the wind on her face, she'll take a deep breath and make a little "Aaah!" sound. I love that we get to spend a lot of time out there on the deck, just enjoying the fresh air. When we're looking out over the railings, it's just the four of us together as a family, with nothing to distract us but the view!

—Christiana Coleman, Isabella and Chloe's Mom

Conner, 1 ½ years
The Morris Family
Texas

Green Thumb

My son Conner loves to garden. He's been helping me and my husband Chris take care of our garden since he was able to walk! He's always loved to be outside with our family. Conner's favorite activity is watering the plants. When he was younger, he used the hose, but now he's old enough to carry the watering pail. The spout is about as big as he is, but he loves it. Conner is already prepared for his first summer job, that will start in about 15 years! He's all boy and loves everything about being outdoors. Seeing how happy it makes him always brings a smile to my face.
—Amanda Morris, Bailey and Conner's Mom

Izaan, 1 ½ years
The Mujahid Family
Pennsylvania

Home Team

I've been playing soccer since I was four years old. My dad taught me the sport and I have passed it on to my children Izaan and Shaira. Sometimes I watch soccer on TV with Izaan. As soon as he sees the ball on the screen he gets excited and he'll yell at the players on TV and say, "Kick! Kick!" Izaan and I love watching soccer, but we love playing it together even more! After work, when my wife Shamila and I come home, we all goof around with a ball in the living room as a family. It's during moments like this that I treasure the game of soccer and the bond it has created between me and my kids.

—Asim Mujahid, Shaira and Izaan's Dad

Little Miss Mommy

Addison is very much the big sister and likes to be Little Miss Mommy to her younger brother Jackson. Now that Addison is old enough to hold Jackson, that's all she ever wants to do! Addison is a very nurturing little girl. When Jackson was born, she started playing "baby" with her dolls, taking care of them just like I take care of Jackson.

Addison loves being a big sister, and she loves doing things for "her" Jack just as much as she likes to take care of her dolls. The two are always playing together. Addison loves giving Jackson kisses and Jackson loves laughing at the silly things Addison does. My husband Damon and I knew that from day one Addison and Jackson would be our whole world, but we didn't anticipate the joy we would get out of seeing Addison's world revolve around her little brother Jackson, too!
—Angie Hummel, Addison and Jackson's Mom

Beach Bound

After 9/11, my husband William re-enlisted in the military and we moved to Hawaii. We adopted Emmie last year from a local Hawaiian woman, so we try to keep her in touch with the Hawaiian culture and spend as much time as possible at the beach with our friends from the island. Emmie loves interacting with all the people, the wind blowing on her face and wearing her little sunglasses while I take photos of her playing with her dad. This child has brought so much joy, not just into our lives, but into the lives of our family and our friends as well. We are truly blessed in having Emmie.

I know that everyone loves and appreciates their children. But when you have to work harder for something, you tend to appreciate it a little more. When Emmie laughs, or even when she cries, I just tell myself how lucky I am to have her in my life.
— April Hand, Emmie's Mom

Brighton, 2 years
The Henrichsen Family
Oregon

Funhouse

Recently we took our son Brighton to an inflatable play center in Portland. He had a blast! Now we try to go as often as we can to spend time together. Brighton loves bouncing in the castle and going down the slides with us. My wife Tara and I get in the bouncy houses and jump around with him. Brighton loves to explore the place; he goes through a little obstacle course and tunnel to get to the slide. Tara and I love spending quality time with our son, especially when it means we all get to jump around and act like kids together!
—Nicole Henrichsen, Brighton's Mom

Baby Bookworm

Nico was born 10 weeks premature and spent a little over a month in the NICU. During that time we weren't allowed to hold him. He was just so tiny: his whole hand was the length of one joint on my finger. The hardest part about Nico being in the NICU was leaving the hospital every night and not being able to take him home with us.

Now that he's home, we love just holding him because we weren't able to for so long. I'm home with him during the day, and then when my husband Tom comes home at night, we both sing a song at bedtime and read him a story. The story and singing have always calmed Nico, even when he was very little. The ritual soothes him and lets him know that it's time for bed. When we used to visit Nico in the hospital in the evenings, we would sing to him before we said goodnight. Now that Nico is at home and doing well, Tom and I still enjoy reading Nico a story and singing before every bedtime.

—Lena Mucchetti, Nico's Mom

Kaden, 1 year
The Colville Family
New Hampshire

Taste Tester

I've been making cakes since I was 14. I attended cooking school, and a year after Kaden was born, I started my own business. I get to spend a lot of time with Kaden since I work from home. He's always in the kitchen with me. I'll give him a plastic bowl and spoon and he pretends that he's stirring. It's so cute to watch him pretend to bake. Kaden is my little taste tester. His expressions are the most honest opinions of my cakes that I get! I love to see his face covered in icing and smiling up at me. I'm so thankful that I can work from home and spend so much quality time with my son.

—Ashlee Colville, Kaden's Mom

Doctor in the House

I am a home health nurse; I started the business so that I could bring my daughters Kendall and Katelynn to work with me. I love being able to have them with me every day and my patients love it too! While the girls are with me, they watch me use my stethoscope to check the patients' chests and bellies, and to take blood pressure. When Kendall figured out how the stethoscope worked, she started to take mine and mimic what I do at work.

My husband Jay and I got her a toy stethoscope and a little medical kit of her own, and now she plays doctor with her little sister all the time. She'll ask, "Is Katelynn sick?" then listen to her baby sister's belly. I'll ask her, "What do you hear?" and she'll say, "I hear bubbles!" Katelynn giggles and laughs when Kendall examines her. It has truly strengthened the bond I have with my daughters to spend this time with them. I know it might be too early, but I can't wait to see my girls grow up to be doctors and surgeons!
—Lacey Byers, Kendall and Katelynn's Mom

Grace, 1 year
The Shaughnessy Family
Nebraska

Ladies on the Lake

My grandmother, Grace's great-grandmother, lives next to a lake just outside of Omaha. The whole family spends most of our holidays at the lake and my husband Ryan and I were even married there. Needless to say, the place has a lot of sentimental value to me, and I love being able to bring my daughter there. Grace and I like to walk around on the beach and put our feet in the water. Going out on the little dock is her favorite thing to do. The lake house has always been a special place, but it's even more special now that I get to experience it with my daughter.
—Michelle Shaughnessy, Grace's Mom

Armstrong Twins, 1 year
The Armstrong Family
North Carolina

Girl Group

On top of being a full-time nurse, I'm a single mom, so my days are long and exhausting. At the end of a long shift, I can't wait to come home to my twins, Brooke and Lynn. I try to spend as much time as possible with my girls to make up for the time we're apart. The girls love music—they dance and sing along to whatever is on TV or the radio. Brooke and Lynn each have a little microphone that they sing into and I will grab a hairbrush and sing right along with them. They are like two little entertainers. All three of us sing and dance all over the house— it's like a concert right there in our living room!
—Stephanie Posey, Brooke and Lynn's Mom

Audrey, 2 years
The Grunow Family
Montana

Masterpiece

Audrey loves to finger paint. She's very dainty; she makes little dots and lines with her fingertips. I often play music while we paint and she will make squiggles in time to the music. My husband Peter and I love to watch her painting, to see her understand what happens when she mixes colors. It's also great to watch her put paint on her whole hand and make a handprint on the paper. Sometimes she even paints her belly or her face! Right now, it's all about the colors for her. Even though it can get messy, the goal is to have fun and explore. The end result doesn't matter so much.
—Frances Grunow, Audrey's Mom

Apple Pie

In the 1940s, my great-grandfather bought 900 acres of land in Iowa. The farm has been in the family for five generations and my parents live there now. My mother and I both grew up in the farmhouse, took walks in the ravine, and played with the animals. That's something I want to share with my son Cruz as he gets older. My husband Luis, Cruz, and I live about 15 minutes from the farm and we take advantage of every moment we can be there. Sunday evenings are a time for the whole family to get together. There are apple trees all over the farm, so my mom and I whip up apple pie together for the family to enjoy. Cruz is getting old enough to start eating pie, and he really likes how sweet it is!

Spending time together is a welcome end to the workweek. Sunday dinners on the farm are a huge part of our lives. Luis and I are always busy and sometimes it seems like our cell phones are ringing non-stop. These dinners are a time for us to put down our phones, laugh, and talk together without distractions. We want to make sure that Cruz knows the value of family and can enjoy the little things we do together as he grows up. I look forward to Sunday dinners with Cruz and my family every week!
—Beth Trejo, Cruz's Mom

Preslee, 1 ½ years
The Wilson Family
South Dakota

Whoaaa Baby

Nichole and I like to take our three kids to a play center in town that has inflatable toys, obstacle courses, slides and bounce houses. When we're there, we try to get the whole family to play together. Preslee, our youngest, loves the play place and the slides are her favorite. She'll go down on the slide, and always let out a big "WHOAAAA" as she slides down. Her older brother and sister, Rylee and Marlee, love to play with Preslee in the bounce houses. We all love seeing Preslee's face light up when we make her laugh as we play together.

—Brian Wilson; Rylee, Marlee, and Preslee's Dad

Charleen, 10 months
The Brown Family
Wisconsin

Copycat

Charleen loves to imitate everything I do. When I finish combing my hair, she picks up the comb and tries to brush her own hair with it. Her favorite thing to do is to play with my phone and pretend to text like I do. Whenever I put my phone down, she picks it up and starts to push the buttons. She also has three older siblings, and she copies everything they do as well. The older kids are always playing with her and teaching her new things. This is great for her development because she has picked up a lot from them. We all love our little copycat!

—Colleen Brown; Kya, Kaleelah, Eddie Jr., and Charleen's Mom

Tea Party

During the week I go to work and my wife Chilly stays home with our daughter Lilly, so weekend mornings are a chance for us all to spend time together. One Saturday morning, I was making a cappuccino for myself and decided to make a chocolate one for Chilly. I carried it over to her and said, "Here's a mocha," and Lilly immediately asked for one, too! From then on, Lilly has started off her weekend mornings with a cup of hot chocolate with frothed milk, or, as she calls it, a "mok-ya." She looks so cute with the milk all over her upper lip that I can't help smiling.

Lilly also likes to throw afternoon tea parties on the weekends. She has them with her dolls and stuffed animals, with Chilly and me, or with guests that come to the house. Using her miniature tea set, she pours everyone make-believe tea and says, "Cheers!" Just because it's a tea party doesn't mean you are drinking tea; Lilly will announce to the party what they're drinking—sometimes it's tea, sometimes it's even "mok-yas!" I know every parent feels this way about their kids, but Lilly is such a joy. It's a good thing she's a daddy's girl, because I can't get enough of her!
                    —Brian Goodman, Lilly's Dad

Baby Girl, Due in July
The Covey Family
New York

Mommy-to-be

Jason and I like to go for long walks together around the city. We're both musicians and work in the evenings, so we're able to enjoy the daytime together. Lately we've been talking a lot about our baby girl, who is due in three months, and how much our lives are going to change when she arrives. Jason often leans down and talks to my belly. He tells her that we can't wait to meet her and that she's already loved. For the rest of our lives we will have another person to care for and it will be both a challenge and a blessing. We're eagerly awaiting her arrival!

—Laura Covey, Expectant Mom

Aayden, 2 years
The Quinn Family
Ohio

Car Crazy

My son Aayden became obsessed with his toy cars when he was about a year old. During playtime, he drifts off into his own little imaginary world and lines the cars up like they're in a parking lot, or in traffic jams all over the house. Aayden often points out something new about the cars, like the headlights, and I'll laugh wondering where he learned it from! When you have kids, you learn to expect the unexpected. Those unpredictible moments bring me so much happiness—they're the best part of my day.
—Lelana Quinn, Aayden's Mom

Caleb, 1 year
The Davila Family
Massachusetts

Bilingual Baby

My husband Rafael and I always look forward to the evenings after work when we can spend time together with Caleb. All three of us sit around, play patty–cake, and learn together as a family. We want Caleb to speak both English and Spanish, so we are trying to teach him words in both languages. If my husband says, "Give mama a hug," I say the same in Spanish. Then I'll tell him to give his father a hug. Caleb loves to go back and forth between us, giving us hugs and kisses. He gets all excited, claps, and says, "Yay!" because he sees how happy it makes us.
—Elouise Davila, Caleb's Mom

Mia, 1 ½ years
The Pierce Family
Maine

Shopping Spree

Mia loves to go to our local organic food store. They have a shopping cart that's just her size and it's adorable to watch her push it through the aisles. When Mia knows where something is, she heads right toward it. A lot of the produce is at her level, which introduces her to different foods, colors, and textures. Every once in a while, there will be a fruit or vegetable that she doesn't recognize and it's a good opportunity for me to teach her its name. The most wonderful sense of joy I experience is being able to see things through Mia's eyes. It's an incredible experience and a gift to see the world through the eyes of a child.
—Jennifer Nadeau, Mia's Mom

Addison, 10 months
The Arroyo Family
Illinois

Staying Connected

As a working mom, I try to spend as much of my free time with my daughter Addison as I can. She is growing up so fast that if you blink you could miss something! Addison's grandma lives far away, but thanks to video chatting, she doesn't have to miss a beat. Family is important to my husband Peter and me, so we love that our daughter can still spend time with her grandma, even though she can't physically be here all the time. When Addison sees her grandma on the screen, she reaches for her. It is wonderful to see Addison recognize her grandma and get excited when she sees her!

—Jennifer Arroyo, Addison's Mom

111

Meg, 1 ½ years
The McMahon Family
Michigan

Soon-to-be Sister

My husband Bill and I are expecting our second baby in a few weeks and could not be more excited. We talk to our daughter Meg a lot about the baby in my belly, and she knows she'll soon have a new brother or sister. She gets happy and smiley and touches my belly. Since we've been telling Meg about her new brother or sister, she has become very aware of babies, and will point them out at church or when we're out and about. We're hoping she'll be just as thrilled when we bring home our new bundle of joy. For now, Bill and I enjoy watching her curiosity grow.

—Kristy McMahon, Meg's Mom

Cadence, 2 years
The Johnson Family
Missouri

Snuggle Up

We decided to have kids while we were young, since we wanted to have plenty of energy to chase them around. Thank goodness we did! With three young kids, me in school full-time, and my husband Bryan on call 24/7 as a locksmith, we're a busy family. The most precious moment of our day is when we all get together on the sofa. We cuddle, play games, watch TV, and unwind. Sometimes we all end up dog piling on top of Daddy. When we're all together, it feels like all is right in the world and we can finally relax.

—Kelly Johnson; Jayden, Alexas, and Cadence's Mom

Little Greeter

Both my husband Rashawn and I work full-time, and although the hours are sometimes grueling, it's even harder to be away from our children all day. So when either of us comes home, we're in for a real treat! Our youngest, Taylor, is always so excited when Rashawn or I walk through the front door. When he hears the door open, he is up and running to get picked up for a big hug. If my hands are full and I can't pick him up right away, he'll just grab my leg and hold onto it! Rashawn and I call him, "our little greeter." Once he's in our arms, all we have to say is, "mmmm" and he showers us with kisses. It's so sweet to see how much he misses and loves us.

As parents, sometimes we can get caught up in the whirlwind of life, but our kids are always there to bring us back to what's important. After a long hard day of work, I couldn't think of anything better than coming home to smiles, hugs, and kisses from Taylor!
—April Harris, Kennedy and Taylor's Mom

Erin, 7 months
The Dolan Family
Alabama

Daddy's Girl

Our daughter Erin is a daddy's girl. She and my husband John make each other laugh all the time. They love to stare at each other in mutual admiration, since they look a lot alike. Erin loves it when John plays the guitar and sings for us. I think it's because she heard it in the womb, since John played to her while I was pregnant.

In the evenings, after dinner, the three of us get settled down together and John gets out the guitar. Erin sits close to her daddy and reaches for the guitar to help him strum the strings and drum on the guitar with her hands. She was only about five months old the first time she tried to help John strum, but now she's an essential part to most of the songs! It's like her very own little concert every evening. She's a very captive audience; she's probably the best audience John will ever have. I treasure the time with all of us together at the end of the day.

—Sonya Dolan, Erin's Mom

Time Together

Addyson is our first child and we love just to be with her. We treasure our time with Addyson in the evenings. At dinner time, she gets excited as soon as we wheel out the high chair. If we pause for a moment while feeding her, she bangs her little hand to get our attention—it's the cutest thing! After a bath in her pink tub, we all sit together to play, read books, and snuggle. The highlight of both my day and my wife Amber's is coming home and sitting down for some one-on-one time with Addyson. It makes everything else worthwhile.

—Joseph Spehar, Addyson's Dad

Brandon, 1 ½ years
The Arvizu Family
New Jersey

Monkeying Around

Our whole family goes to Liberty State Park all the time to play on the playground there. Our son Brandon can't reach the monkey bars yet, so my wife Martha and I hold him up so he can grab on, then we help him move from bar to bar. It's so cute to see how accomplished he feels after he's made it to the end! Soon Brandon will be able to do it all on his own, but right now, he still needs our help. He is growing and becoming more independent each day. Going to the park together is a great time for all of us. We love to see Brandon running around being a happy, smiling kid.

—Randy Arvizu, Keneda and Brandon's Dad

Cameron, 3 years
The Cooper Family
Maryland

Family Fun

Bath time is controlled chaos in our house. Kayla, Cameron, and Kelsey have a great time splashing and playing around. When bath time is over, they're off running in a million different directions. Once everybody is dry and dressed, we all gather together in Kayla's room for more fun! Since my husband Corjuan and I work full-time, we take this opportunity to spend quality time with our children—we read stories, laugh, and play games together. I am so amazed to see how the kids are growing and learning. Every day they will say something new, or do something that I've never seen before. Watching this discovery makes parenting so rewarding.

—Erin Cooper; Kayla, Cameron, and Kelsey's Mom

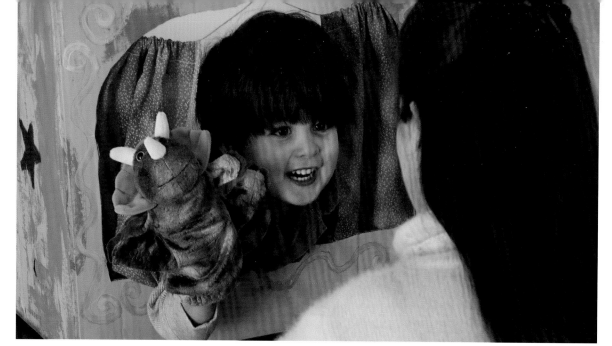

Mihir, 2 years
The Iyer Family
Washington

Puppet Theater

Our boys, Mihir and Kieran, love being creative, doing art projects, and playing make-believe. Mihir looks up to his big brother and wants to do everything with him. He is always ready to follow Kieran's lead. Whether Kieran likes it or not, Mihir is stuck to him like glue! Kieran has a knack for storytelling, so when the boys got puppets from their grandparents as a gift, I decided to make a puppet theater out of a box so they could put on shows together. I love being their audience—it's so amazing to see the two of them play together and to watch their imaginations go wild!

—Elyse Iyer, Kieran and Mihir's Mom

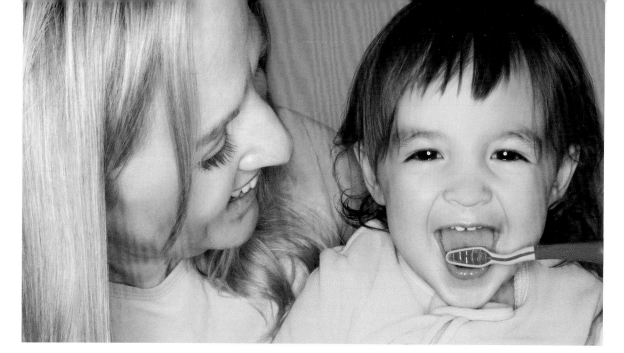

Eliah, 1 ½ years
The Fernandez Family
Colorado

Ready for Bed

For some families, getting ready for bed is a challenge, but in our house, we enjoy every minute with our daughter Eliah! My husband Vinnie is in charge of her bath. When we've finished eating, Eliah knows it's time for a bath and runs over to the tub. Afterwards, she grabs her toothbrush and holds it in her hand, gabbering away instead of brushing her teeth. Eliah hates actually having her teeth brushed, so we make a game of it! We love our nighttime ritual with Eliah. It's exciting to see her know what's next in the routine, and try to do things herself. Vinnie and I treasure the time we spend getting our baby ready for bed.
—Elizabeth Fernandez, Eliah's Mom

Double Kiss

At night, before we put our son Isaiah to bed, my husband David and I always stop what we're doing—dishes, laundry, and everything else that needs to be done—to spend a little family time together. I give Isaiah a bath, wrap him in his little hooded towel, and then tell him, "Go get Daddy!" Isaiah will run through the house to find my husband, grab his favorite blankets, and the three of us will snuggle up on the couch.

Once it's time for bed, David and I both stand up and give Isaiah a kiss at the same time, one of us on each side, to say goodnight and tell him how much we love him. Then, David will pick Isaiah up, take him to bed, and say his prayers with him. Our goodnight kiss unites the three of us and shows Isaiah that he is loved by both of his parents. We started this tradition when he was very little, and it gives him a sense of security, even though we're putting him to bed. Our schedule is hectic and we're always trying to balance a lot of things, but we make the most of the time we have with Isaiah. At the very least, we have these special moments together at bedtime.

—Sarah Kay, Isaiah's Mom

Wacky Hair

James is a fish. He loves the water and he loves bath time. It's never hard to get him into the tub in the evenings because he knows that's his time to play before he goes to bed, so he has it all out in the tub. The hard part is getting him out! Most of the water ends up outside the tub, all over me and the walls. He loves to splash around and play with toys. When I shampoo his hair, I play with it. I'll spike it all straight up, shape two horns on the sides, or make a little mohawk. Once I'm finished, I pour the water over his head to get all the shampoo out.

I had always wanted to have a family, but was told that I would never be able to have children. James is my miracle baby. Both my husband Guillermo and I work and leaving him at day care is hard. He's such a blessing; I try to treasure every moment I have with him. I love soaking up those fun moments in the tub.
—Sylvia Miranda, James' Mom

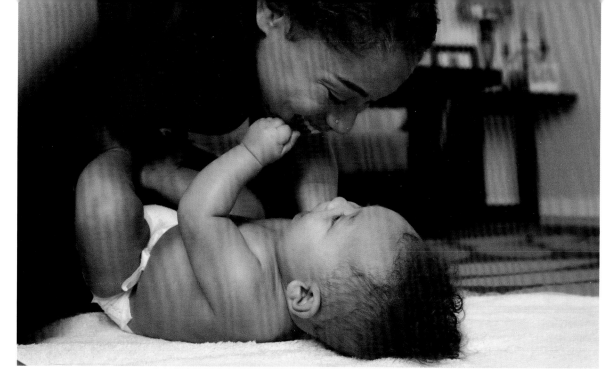

Kayden, 5 months
The Rogers Family
New Mexico

Rock-a-bye Baby

Nighttime is one more chance for me to bond with my son Kayden. I hold him tightly up to my chest as we sit in a rocking chair in his room, rocking back and forth until he is almost asleep. It's a special time for just Kayden and I. We're fortunate to have a lot of family members who live close by, so Kayden is surrounded by company in the daytime. Everyone is excited to play with him and hold him. I joke that when we visit family, I don't get to see him again until we leave! This makes those quiet moments alone together in the evening all the more special. I treasure the opportunity to be close with my son and get to know him better.
—Emily Rogers, Kayden's Mom

Index

Missouri	116		Pennsylvania	58
The Johnson Family			The Mujahid Family	
Montana	84		Rhode Island	34
The Grunow Family			The Sexton Family	
Nebraska	80		South Carolina	50
The Shaughnessy Family			The Billings Family	
Nevada	8		South Dakota	90
The Buckley Family			The Wilson Family	
New Hampshire	72		Tennessee	42
The Colville Family			The Zuker Family	
New Jersey	126		Texas	56
The Arvizu Family			The Morris Family	
New Mexico	142		Utah	18
The Rogers Family			The Hill Family	
New York	96		Vermont	36
The Covey Family			The Satz Family	
North Carolina	82		Virginia	124
The Armstrong Family			The Spehar Family	
North Dakota	94		Washington	132
The Goodman Family			The Iyer Family	
Ohio	100		West Virginia	136
The Quinn Family			The Kay Family	
Oklahoma	32		Wisconsin	92
The Turner Family			The Brown Family	
Oregon	68		Wyoming	76
The Henrichsen Family			The Byers Family	

Birch Books
328 West 77th Street
New York, NY 10024
birchbooks.com

©Johnson & Johnson Consumer Companies, Inc. 2011
Photographs Copyright 2011
by Michael Franzini

Library of Congress
2011922852

ISBN-10: 0-9845717-1-X
ISBN-13: 978-0-9845717-1-0
Printed in the USA

Designed by Birch Cooper